CHER

A Little Golden Book® Biography

By Candice Ransom • Illustrated by Laura Catrinella

A GOLDEN BOOK • NEW YORK

Golden Books
An imprint of Random House Children's Books
A division of Penguin Random House LLC
1745 Broadway, New York, NY 10019
penguinrandomhouse.com
rhcbooks.com

Library of Congress Control Number: 2024950011
ISBN 979-8-217-02988-4 (trade) — ISBN 979-8-217-02989-1 (ebook)
Manufactured in the United States of America
10 9 8 7 6 5 4 3 2 1
EU Contact: Penguin Random House Ireland, 32 Nassau Street, Dublin D02 YH68.
https://eu-contact.penguin.ie

Cherilyn Sarkisian was born on May 20, 1946, in El Centro, California. Her mother had blond hair and blue eyes, but Cher had black hair and brown eyes like her Armenian American father. Cher's parents divorced when she was a baby. Her mother remarried and had another daughter. Cher's half sister was also blond and blue-eyed. With her dark looks, Cher felt she was different.

When Cher was four years old, her mother took her to see the Disney movie *Dumbo* at Grauman's Chinese Theatre in Hollywood. Cher was amazed by the huge stage and golden curtain that seemed to rise like magic.

The movie was about a small circus elephant who was different from the other elephants. But when Dumbo learned to fly, he became the star of the show. Cher stared at the screen as the animals danced and sang songs. She wanted to do that, too.

At home, Cher would sing all the time. She sang without thinking about it. It was just something she did.

Cher put on a performance of the musical *Oklahoma!* for her fifth-grade class. She taught the songs and dances to some of the girls. None of the boys wanted to be in the show, so Cher acted and sang all their parts.

When she was twelve, she practiced signing her name so she'd be ready to give autographs when she became a famous movie star.

In high school, Cher put her shiny black hair in two ponytails and wore huge sunglasses, just like Audrey Hepburn, her favorite actress. But school was hard for Cher. She'd always had trouble reading. Numbers made no sense to her. She felt different from her classmates.

She decided to follow her dream of being a performer. Cher left school and moved to Hollywood with a friend. She began taking acting lessons and worked in a department store to earn money.

One evening, she was in a coffee shop when a young man with long hair and a big smile walked in. His name was Salvatore Bono, but everyone called him Sonny. Sonny Bono was an assistant record producer and a songwriter.

Cher became friends with Sonny. He believed she would become a famous singer with her distinctive low voice. He wrote a song for her called "I Got You Babe." But Cher felt nervous. She didn't want to sing alone. So Sonny stood next to her and sang a small part. They often faced each other while performing.

"I Got You Babe" was a big hit in 1965. Suddenly, Sonny and Cher were famous! Girls dyed their hair black and wore bell-bottoms and vests to look like Cher.

By 1971, the singing couple had married, become parents, and were the stars of a TV show. *The Sonny and Cher Comedy Hour* ran for four seasons. Cher looked beautiful with her straight, waist-length hair and beaded gowns made by designer Bob Mackie.

Cher was more comfortable performing now.
During this time, she recorded several hit songs
on her own.

When the TV show ended, Sonny and Cher broke up. Cher married again, to rock star Gregg Allman, and had another child. But that marriage didn't last either.

This was an unhappy time for Cher, but she loved being a mom. She and her children roller-skated and rode bikes together. As a single mother, Cher knew she had to work hard to take care of her family. She gave live performances in Las Vegas—sometimes two shows a night. In 1979, she recorded an album of disco songs.

In 1982, she moved to New York City to become an actress. People didn't believe the singer could be a serious actress—Cher proved them wrong! She landed a part in a Broadway play called *Come Back to the 5 & Dime, Jimmy Dean, Jimmy Dean* and later performed the same role in the movie version.

She received an Oscar nomination for her supporting role in *Silkwood*. And in 1988, she won the Oscar for Best Actress for *Moonstruck*. Cher was a movie star at last!

Cher enjoyed acting, but she missed making music. Times had changed since her pop songs and disco records came out. People listened to different music in the 1980s. So Cher became a rock star, wearing a black leather jacket and singing "If I Could Turn Back Time."

She changed music styles again in 1998 with her hit "Believe." The song sold millions of copies and earned Cher her first Grammy Award for Best Dance Recording. She went on a sold-out tour, traveling all over the United States and Europe. When the tour ended, Cher said she didn't want to go on the road again—but she wasn't done performing!

For three years, starting in 2008, Cher performed at the Colosseum at Caesars Palace in Las Vegas. Fans traveled from all over the world to see her.

Cher opened the show by being lowered from the ceiling on a lit gold platform. Acrobats and dancers joined her on the huge stage. She sang while on a boat and in a giant pearl. She changed costumes and wigs seventeen times a night!

Cher was known around the world as the Goddess of Pop. In 2010, she played the owner of a dance club in a movie starring pop singer Christina Aguilera. The film premiered at Grauman's Chinese Theatre, where Cher had seen her first movie sixty years earlier.

Cher was invited to put her hand- and footprints on cement in front of the theater like other famous celebrities have in the past. It was a great honor.

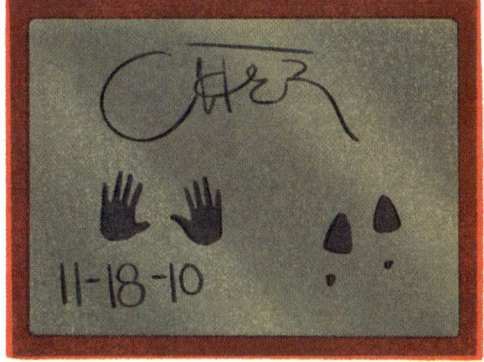

Like Dumbo, Cher was flying high! Ever the star, she sprinkled gold glitter over her cement block.

In 2017, at age seventy, she returned to Las Vegas with a new show. The curtain rose like magic and there was Cher, on top of an enormous mechanical elephant! Dressed in fabulous outfits, as always, she danced and sang for the cheering crowds.

Then a real elephant entered Cher's life. Kaavan had lived in a cramped cell in a zoo in Pakistan for decades. When Cher learned of the animal's plight, she traveled to Pakistan to help rescue the elephant. Thanks to her efforts, and those of other caring people, Kaavan was moved to a wildlife sanctuary in Cambodia. Cher continues working to save other captive wild animals from being mistreated.

Cher has come a long way and done so much. It's no wonder her story was turned into a Broadway musical! *The Cher Show* opened in New York City in 2018. It stars three actresses, playing Cher at different ages and stages of her incredible life.

In 2024, Cher won the iHeartRadio Icon Award. Accepting the award she told the audience, "Have a dream, and don't give it up no matter what happens." Being a performer has always been Cher's dream—and it certainly came true. She is the only female recording artist to have a number one song in each of the last seven decades!

Throughout her career, Cher has had ups and downs. But she never stayed down. She believed in herself and kept finding new ways to entertain people. After more than sixty years in show business, the Goddess of Pop has no plans to stop—and her millions of fans are cheering her on!